"That's all Folks!"

Wabbit Food

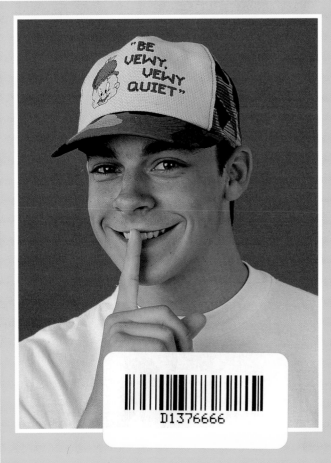

"BE VEWY, VEWY QUIET"

"Sufferin' Succotash"

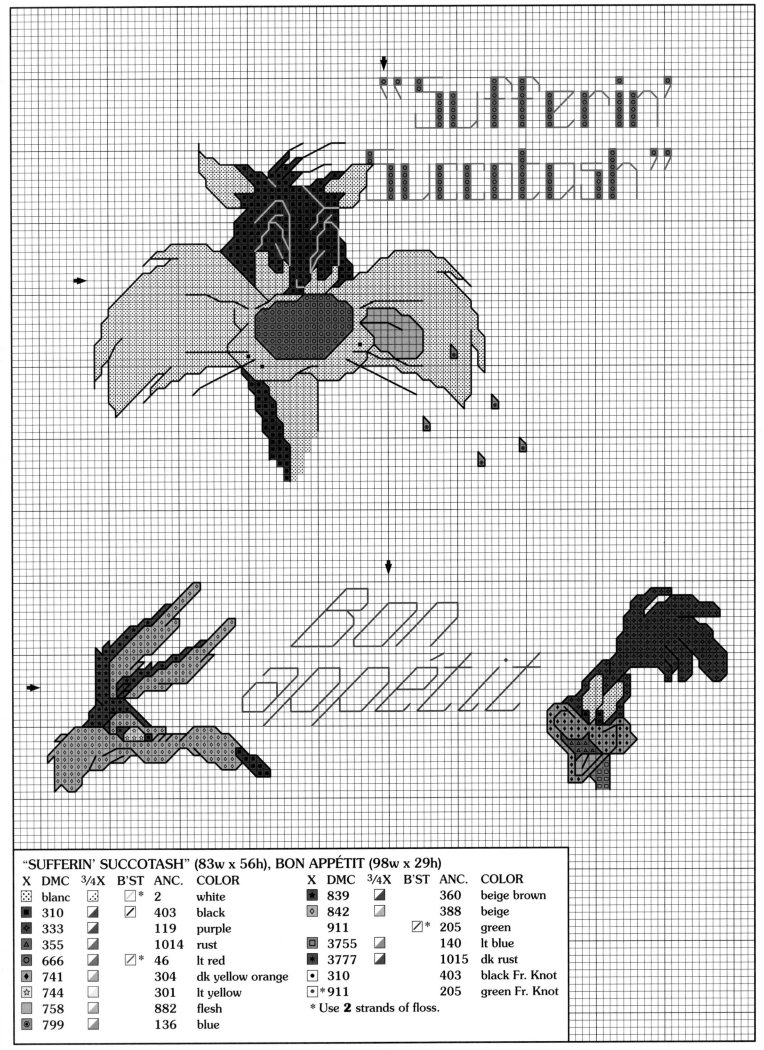

"SUFFERIN' SUCCOTASH" (83w x 56h), BON APPÉTIT (98w x 29h)

X	DMC	¾X	B'ST	ANC.	COLOR		X	DMC	¾X	B'ST	ANC.	COLOR
⊠	blanc	⊡	▧ *	2	white		★	839	◢		360	beige brown
■	310	◢	▧	403	black		◇	842	◢		388	beige
◆	333	◢		119	purple			911		▧ *	205	green
△	355	◢		1014	rust		▣	3755	◢		140	lt blue
◉	666	◢	▧ *	46	lt red		✳	3777	◢		1015	dk rust
◆	741	◢		304	dk yellow orange		•	310			403	black Fr. Knot
☆	744	▢		301	lt yellow		⊙	*911			205	green Fr. Knot
▦	758	◢		882	flesh			* Use **2** strands of floss.				
◉	799	◢		136	blue							

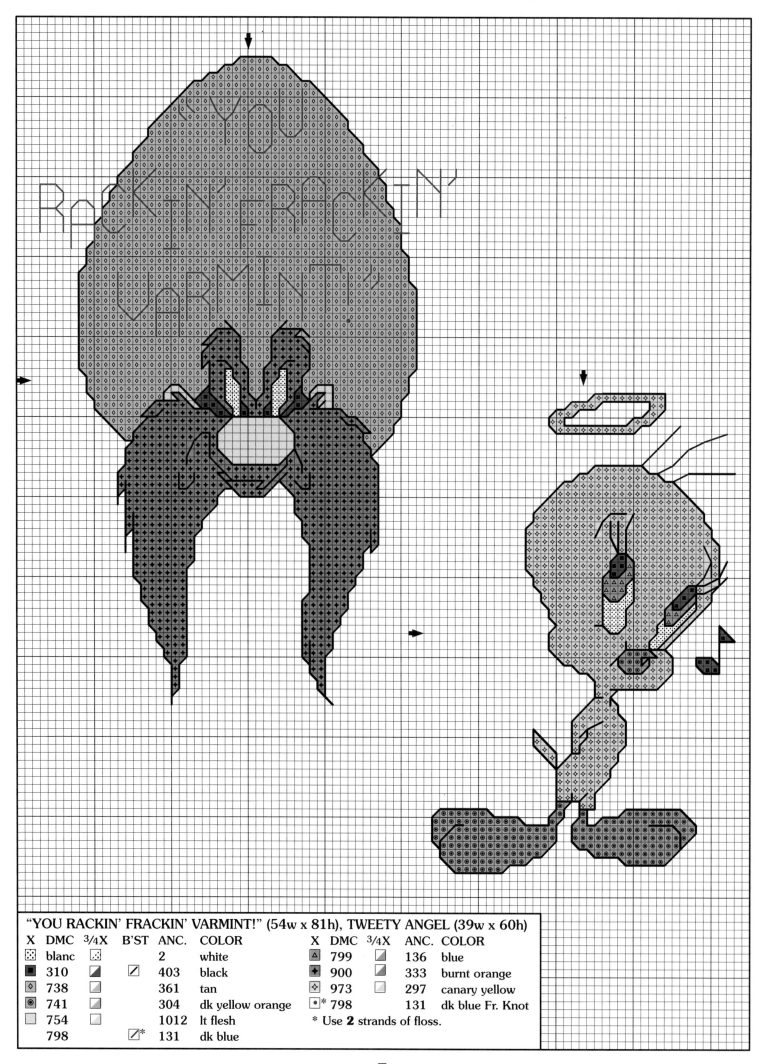

"YOU RACKIN' FRACKIN' VARMINT!" (54w x 81h), TWEETY ANGEL (39w x 60h)

X	DMC	¾X	B'ST	ANC.	COLOR	X	DMC	¾X	ANC.	COLOR
⊠	blanc	⊡		2	white	▲	799	◢	136	blue
■	310	◢	╱	403	black	✚	900	◢	333	burnt orange
◈	738	◢		361	tan	✦	973	◢	297	canary yellow
◉	741	◢		304	dk yellow orange	•*	798		131	dk blue Fr. Knot
▨	754	◻		1012	lt flesh					
	798		╱*	131	dk blue					

* Use **2** strands of floss.

7

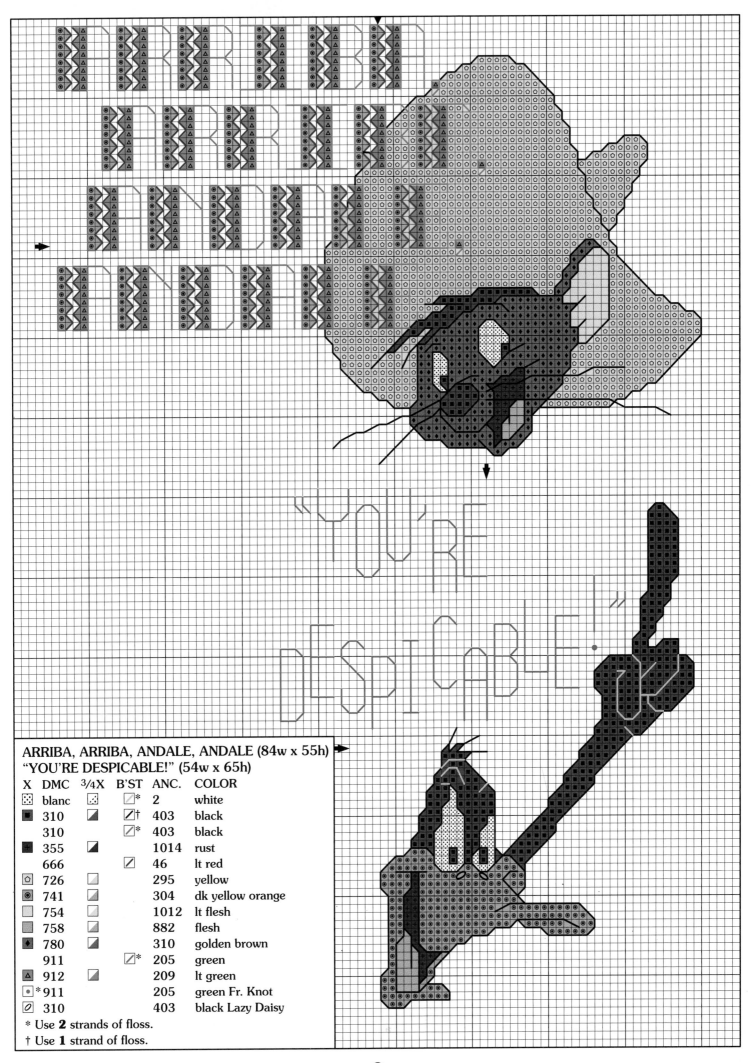

ARRIBA, ARRIBA, ANDALE, ANDALE (84w x 55h)
"YOU'RE DESPICABLE!" (54w x 65h)

X	DMC	¾X	B'ST	ANC.	COLOR
▨	blanc	⬚	◪*	2	white
■	310	◪	◪†	403	black
	310		◪*	403	black
✚	355	◪		1014	rust
	666		◪	46	lt red
⬠	726	◪		295	yellow
◉	741	◪		304	dk yellow orange
▨	754	◪		1012	lt flesh
▨	758	◪		882	flesh
◆	780	◪		310	golden brown
	911		◪*	205	green
▲	912	◪		209	lt green
⊙*	911			205	green Fr. Knot
◪	310			403	black Lazy Daisy

* Use **2** strands of floss.
† Use **1** strand of floss.

8

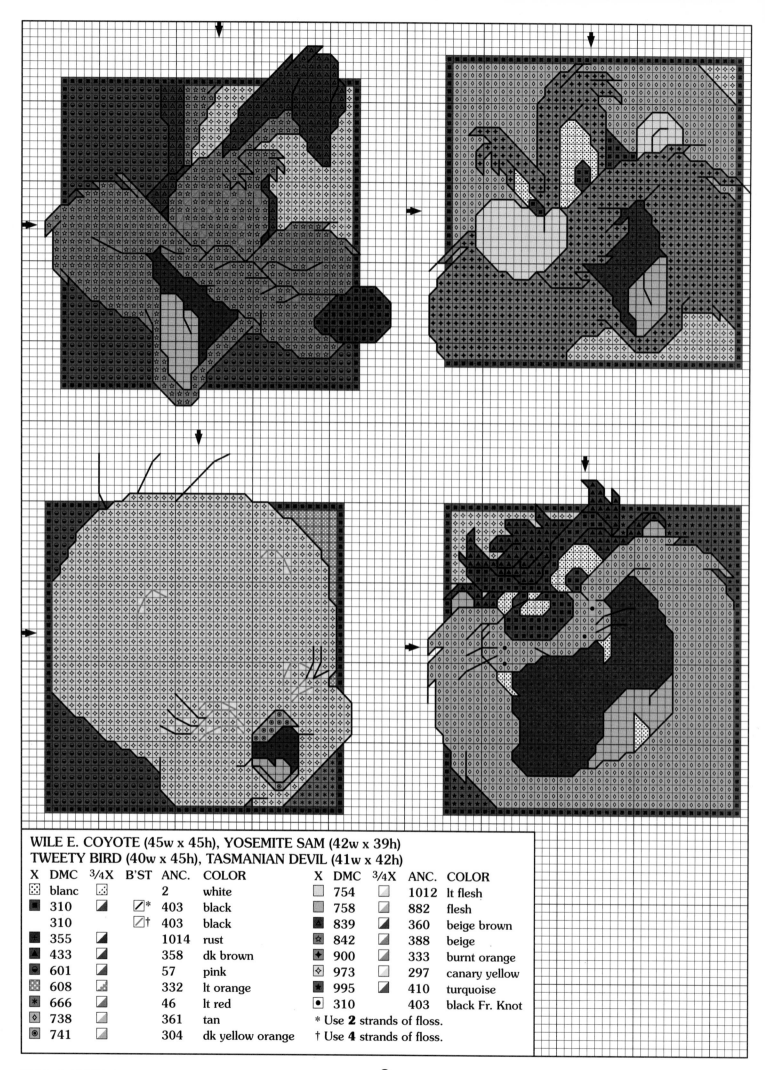

WILE E. COYOTE (45w x 45h), YOSEMITE SAM (42w x 39h)
TWEETY BIRD (40w x 45h), TASMANIAN DEVIL (41w x 42h)

X	DMC	3/4X	B'ST	ANC.	COLOR		X	DMC	3/4X	ANC.	COLOR
⊡	blanc	⊡		2	white			754	◪	1012	lt flesh
■	310	◪	◪*	403	black			758	◪	882	flesh
	310	◪	◪†	403	black		▲	839	◪	360	beige brown
⊞	355	◪		1014	rust		☆	842	◪	388	beige
▲	433	◪		358	dk brown		◆	900	◪	333	burnt orange
⊟	601	◪		57	pink		◇	973	◪	297	canary yellow
▦	608	◪		332	lt orange		★	995	◪	410	turquoise
*	666	◪		46	lt red		●	310		403	black Fr. Knot
◇	738	◪		361	tan						
◉	741	◪		304	dk yellow orange						

* Use **2** strands of floss.
† Use **4** strands of floss.

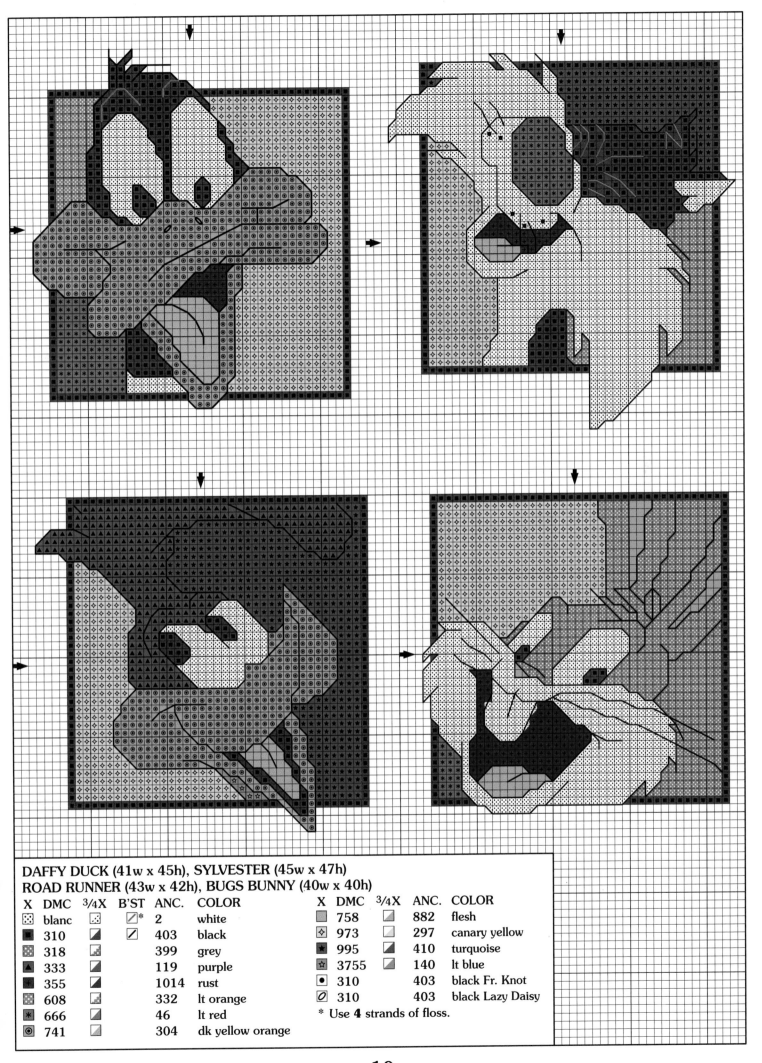

DAFFY DUCK (41w x 45h), SYLVESTER (45w x 47h)
ROAD RUNNER (43w x 42h), BUGS BUNNY (40w x 40h)

X	DMC	¾X	B'ST	ANC.	COLOR
▨	blanc	⊡	◪*	2	white
■	310	◪	◪	403	black
▨	318	◪		399	grey
▲	333	◪		119	purple
✚	355	◪		1014	rust
▨	608	◪		332	lt orange
✳	666	◪		46	lt red
◉	741	◪		304	dk yellow orange

X	DMC	¾X	ANC.	COLOR
▨	758	◪	882	flesh
✧	973	◪	297	canary yellow
★	995	◪	410	turquoise
☆	3755	◪	140	lt blue
●	310		403	black Fr. Knot
⊘	310		403	black Lazy Daisy

* Use **4** strands of floss.

TASMANIAN DEVIL "SOCCER!!" (87w x 73h), TASMANIAN DEVIL "BASEBALL?" (102w x 37h)

X	DMC	¾X	B'ST	ANC.	COLOR	X	DMC	¾X	ANC.	COLOR	X	DMC	¾X	ANC.	COLOR
▨	blanc	⬚		2	white	✚	355	◣	1014	rust		758	◩	882	flesh
▪	310	◣	◿*	403	black	▲	433	◣	358	dk brown	▲	911	◩	205	green
	310		◿†	403	black	◉	436	◪	1045	lt brown	•	310		403	black Fr. Knot
✦	321			9046	red	◈	738	◩	361	tan					
✳	333			119	purple	▦	754	◩	1012	lt flesh					

* Use **2** strands of floss.
† Use **4** strands of floss.

11

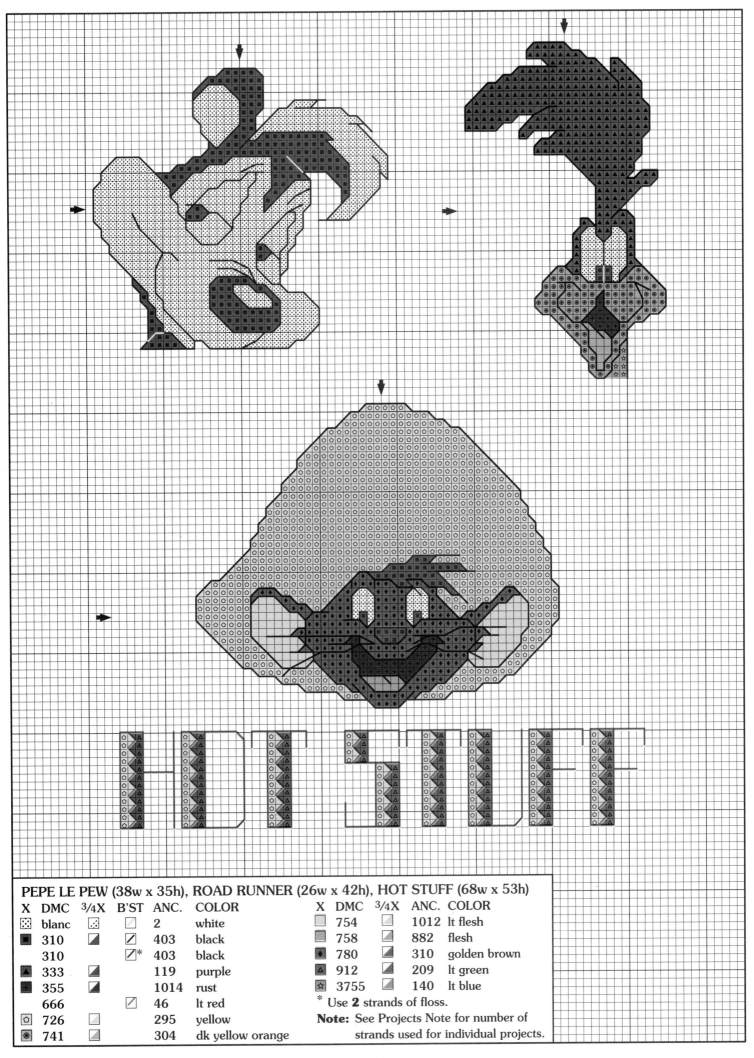

PEPE LE PEW (38w x 35h), ROAD RUNNER (26w x 42h), HOT STUFF (68w x 53h)

X	DMC	¾X	B'ST	ANC.	COLOR	X	DMC	¾X	ANC.	COLOR
▨	blanc	▨	◪	2	white		754	◪	1012	lt flesh
■	310	◪	◪	403	black		758	◪	882	flesh
	310		◪*	403	black	◆	780	◪	310	golden brown
▲	333	◪		119	purple	△	912	◪	209	lt green
✚	355	◪		1014	rust	☆	3755	◪	140	lt blue
	666		◪	46	lt red	* Use **2** strands of floss.				
⬠	726			295	yellow	**Note:** See Projects Note for number of				
◉	741			304	dk yellow orange	strands used for individual projects.				

TWEETY (28w x 38h), SYLVESTER JR. (39w x 34h), PORKY PIG (31w x 32h)
FOGHORN LEGHORN (26w x 42h), "WHAT'S UP, DOC?" (56w x 80h)

X	DMC	¾X	B'ST	ANC.	COLOR	X	DMC	¾X	ANC.	COLOR	X	DMC	¾X	ANC.	COLOR
	blanc			2	white		741		304	dk yellow orange		973		297	canary yellow
	310			403	black		742		303	yellow orange		3777		1015	dk rust
	310		*	403	black		754		1012	lt flesh		310		403	black Fr. Knot
	318			399	grey		758		882	flesh	*	310		403	black Fr. Knot
	355			1014	rust		799		136	blue		310		403	black Lazy Daisy
	666			46	lt red		900		333	burnt orange					

* Use **2** strands of floss.

TASMANIAN DEVIL "STUFF IT!" (90w x 92h)

X	DMC	3/4X	B'ST	ANC.	COLOR	X	DMC	3/4X	ANC.	COLOR
⊠	blanc	⊡		2	white	⊡	742	◪	303	yellow orange
■	310	◪	╱	403	black	-	743	◪	302	lt yellow orange
✳	333	◪		119	purple	▨	754	◪	1012	lt flesh
✚	355	◪		1014	rust	▨	758	◪	882	flesh
▲	433	◪		358	dk brown	◈	946	◪	332	orange
◇	738	◪		361	tan	•	310		403	black Fr. Knot

14

TASMANIAN DEVIL "BLITZ!" (91w x 82h)				
X DMC	3/4X	B'ST	ANC.	COLOR
blanc		*	2	white
310			403	black
355			1014	rust
433			358	dk brown
434			310	brown
738			361	tan
754			1012	lt flesh
758			882	flesh
911			205	green
310			403	black Fr. Knot

*Use **4** strands of floss (long stitches).

15

"THAT'S ALL FOLKS!"(84w x 52h), "WHAT'S COOKIN', DOC?" (89w x 43h)

X	DMC	¾X	B'ST	ANC.	COLOR	X	DMC	¾X	B'ST	ANC.	COLOR
⊞	blanc	⊡		2	white	▨	758	◪		882	flesh
▪	310	◩	◸	403	black		798		◸*	131	dk blue
▽	318	◪		399	grey	⊙*	666			46	lt red Fr. Knot
✚	355	◪		1014	rust	⊙*	798			131	dk blue Fr. Knot
✳	666	◪	◸*	46	lt red	⊘	310			403	black Lazy Daisy
▨	754	◪		1012	lt flesh		* Use **2** strands of floss.				

"BE VEWY, VEWY QUIET"

"I Tawt I Taw A Puddy Tat!"

"BE VEWY, VEWY QUIET" (63w x 38h), "I TAWT I TAW A PUDDY TAT!" (81w x 56h)

X	DMC	¾X	B'ST	ANC.	COLOR	X	DMC	¾X	ANC.	COLOR
▦	blanc	▦		2	white	▢	754	◩	1012	lt flesh
▪	310	◪	╱	403	black	▨	758	◩	882	flesh
✦	321	◪		9046	red	△	799	◩	136	blue
✚	355	◪		1014	rust	◈	973	◩	297	canary yellow
★	434	◪	╱*	310	brown	•†	666		46	lt red Fr. Knot
	666		╱†	46	lt red					
▼	741	◩		304	dk yellow orange					

* Use **4** strands of floss.

† Use **2** strands of floss.

17

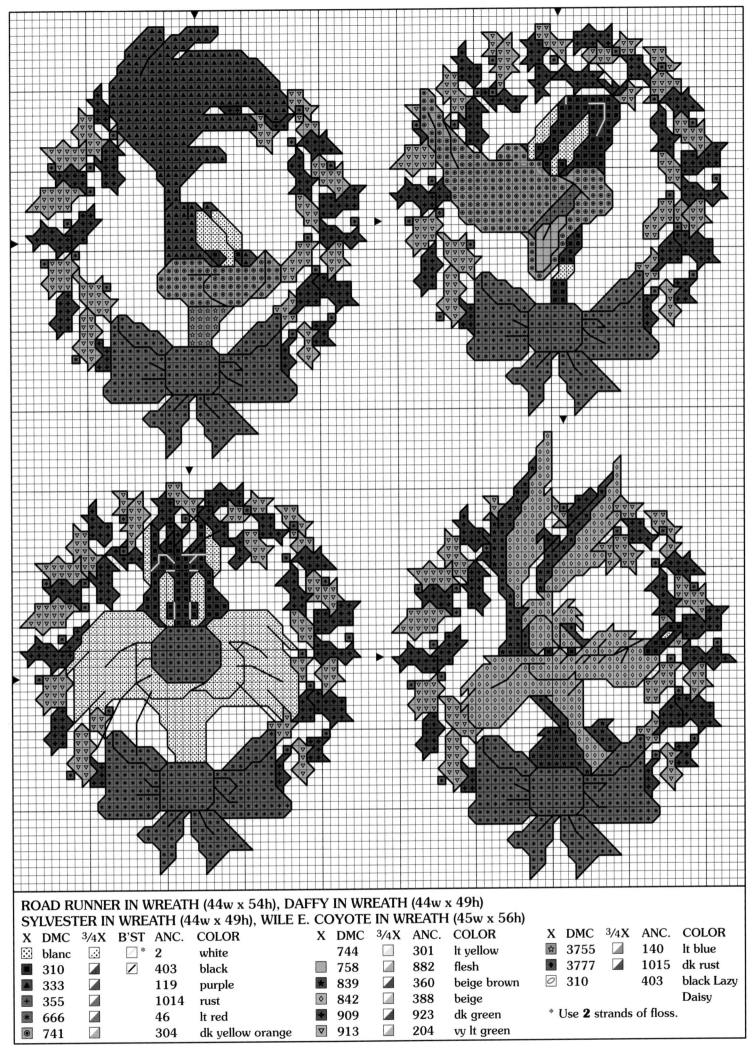

ROAD RUNNER IN WREATH (44w x 54h), DAFFY IN WREATH (44w x 49h)
SYLVESTER IN WREATH (44w x 49h), WILE E. COYOTE IN WREATH (45w x 56h)

X	DMC	¾X	B'ST	ANC.	COLOR	X	DMC	¾X	ANC.	COLOR	X	DMC	¾X	ANC.	COLOR
▨	blanc	▨	☐ *	2	white		744	◪	301	lt yellow	☆	3755	◪	140	lt blue
■	310	◪	◪	403	black		758	◪	882	flesh	✦	3777	◪	1015	dk rust
▲	333	◪		119	purple	✳	839	◪	360	beige brown	⊘	310		403	black Lazy
✚	355	◪		1014	rust	◇	842	◪	388	beige					Daisy
✻	666	◪		46	lt red	✦	909	◪	923	dk green	* Use **2** strands of floss.				
⊙	741	◪		304	dk yellow orange	▽	913	◪	204	vy lt green					

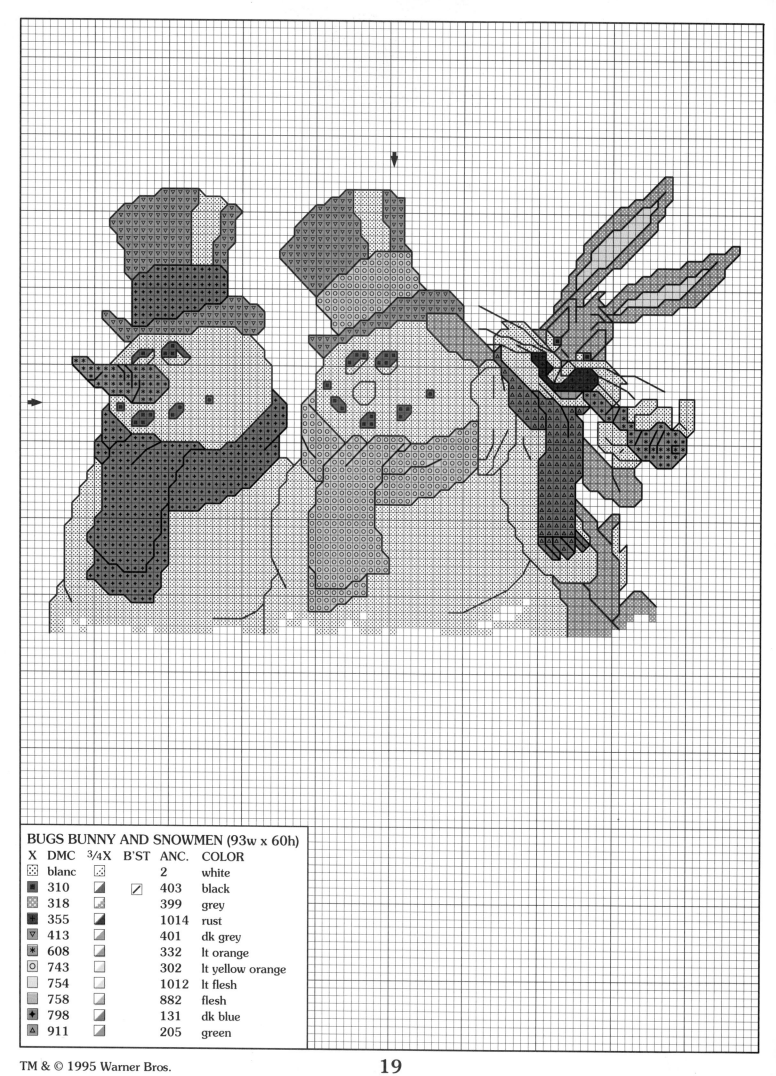

BUGS BUNNY AND SNOWMEN (93w x 60h)

X	DMC	¾X	B'ST	ANC.	COLOR
▨	blanc	▨		2	white
■	310	◩	╱	403	black
▨	318	◩		399	grey
✚	355	◩		1014	rust
▽	413	◩		401	dk grey
✱	608	◩		332	lt orange
⊙	743	◩		302	lt yellow orange
	754	◩		1012	lt flesh
▨	758	◩		882	flesh
✦	798	◩		131	dk blue
△	911	◩		205	green

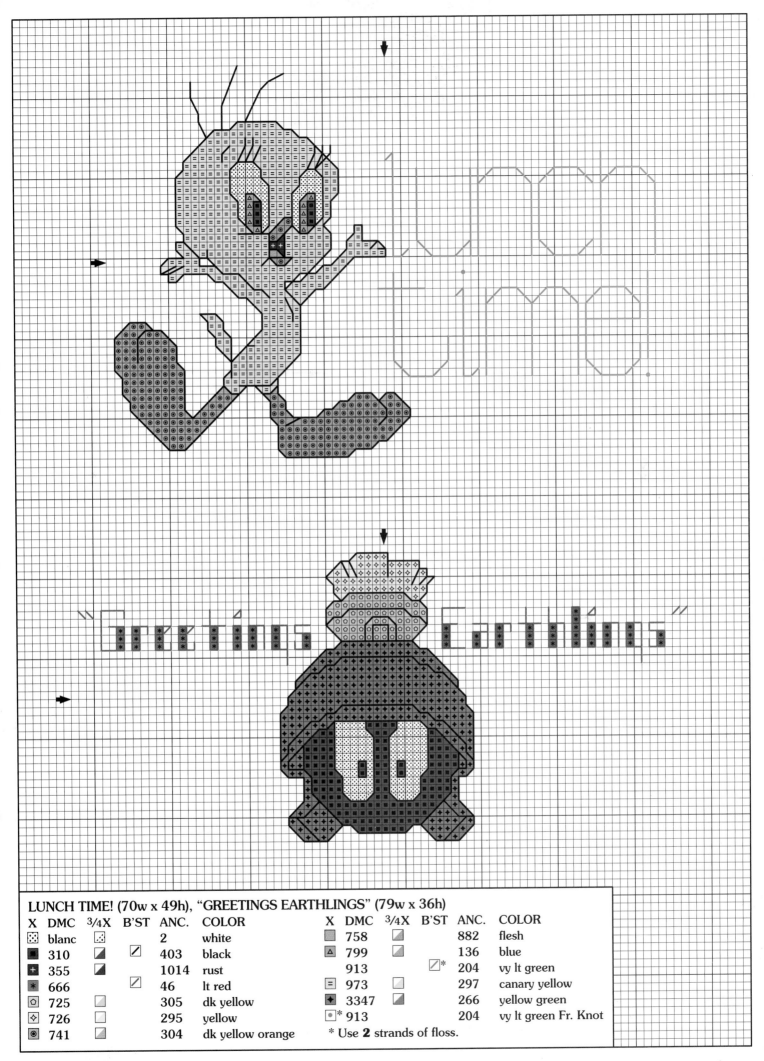

LUNCH TIME! (70w x 49h), "GREETINGS EARTHLINGS" (79w x 36h)

X	DMC	¾X	B'ST	ANC.	COLOR	X	DMC	¾X	B'ST	ANC.	COLOR
▨	blanc	⊡		2	white	▨	758	◰		882	flesh
■	310	◹	⟋	403	black	△	799	◰		136	blue
✚	355	◹		1014	rust		913		⟋*	204	vy lt green
✳	666		⟋	46	lt red	=	973	◰		297	canary yellow
⬠	725	◰		305	dk yellow	✦	3347	◰		266	yellow green
✧	726	◰		295	yellow	⊙*	913			204	vy lt green Fr. Knot
◉	741	◰		304	dk yellow orange		*Use **2** strands of floss.				

20

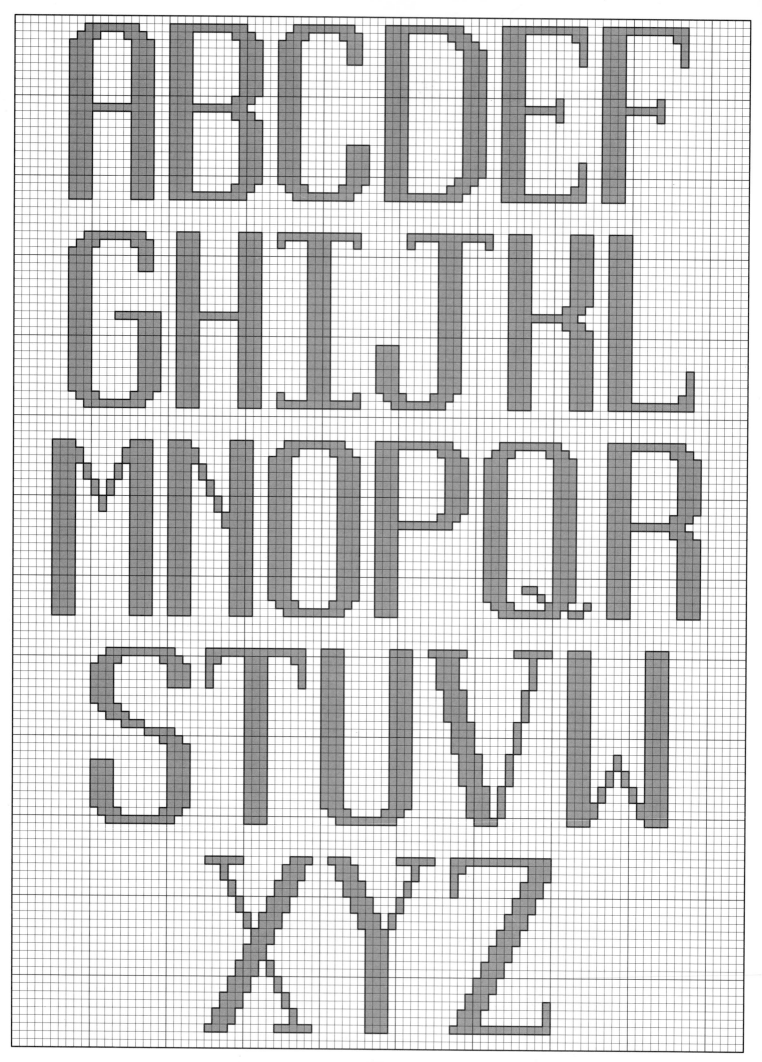